Happy 1978!

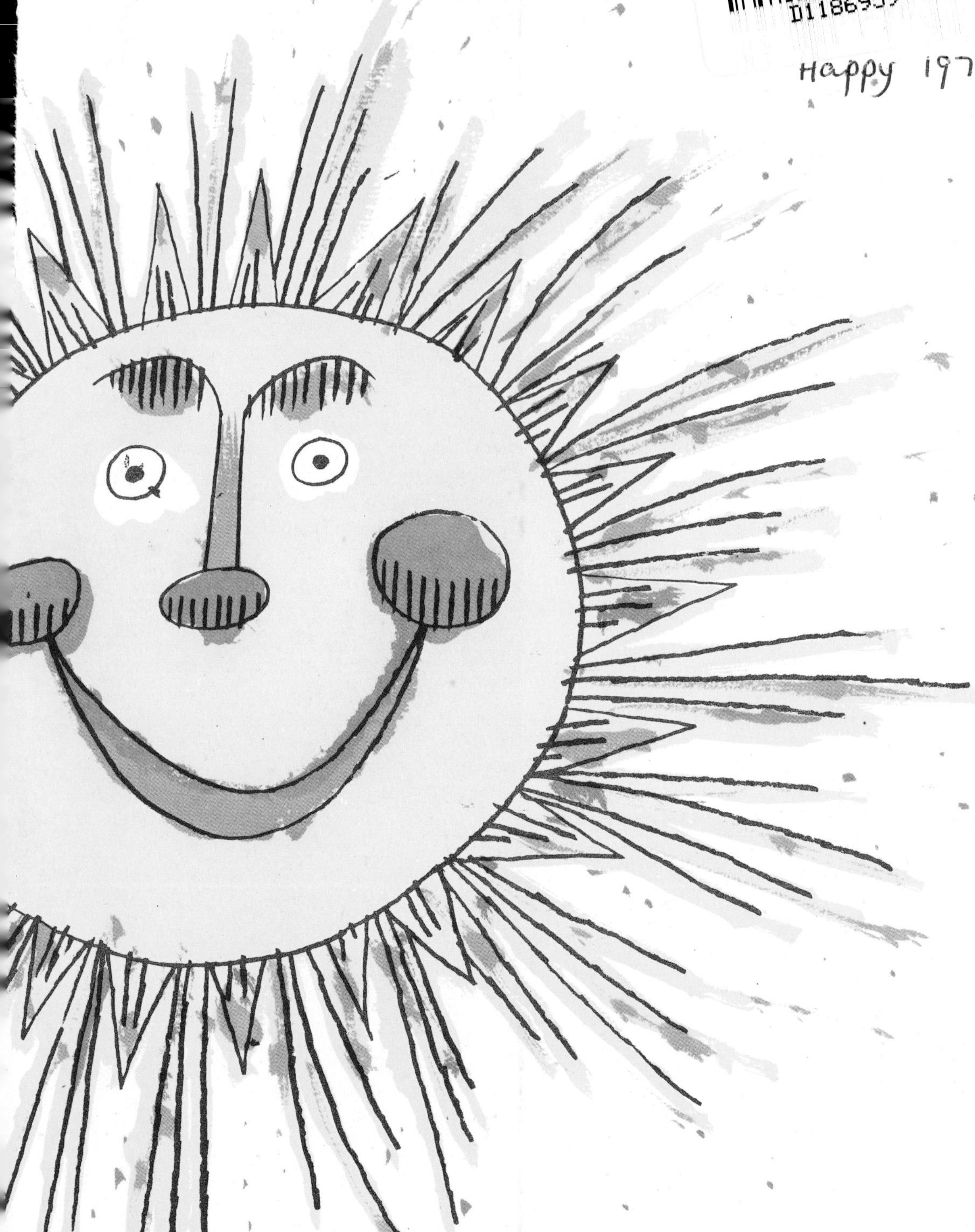

Richard Scarry's
BEST STORY
BOOK EVER

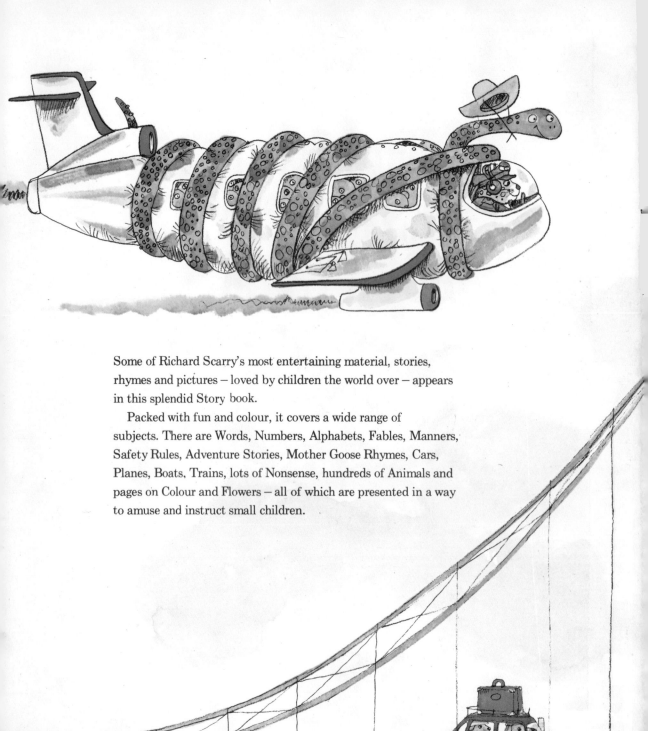

Some of Richard Scarry's most entertaining material, stories, rhymes and pictures – loved by children the world over – appears in this splendid Story book.

Packed with fun and colour, it covers a wide range of subjects. There are Words, Numbers, Alphabets, Fables, Manners, Safety Rules, Adventure Stories, Mother Goose Rhymes, Cars, Planes, Boats, Trains, lots of Nonsense, hundreds of Animals and pages on Colour and Flowers – all of which are presented in a way to amuse and instruct small children.

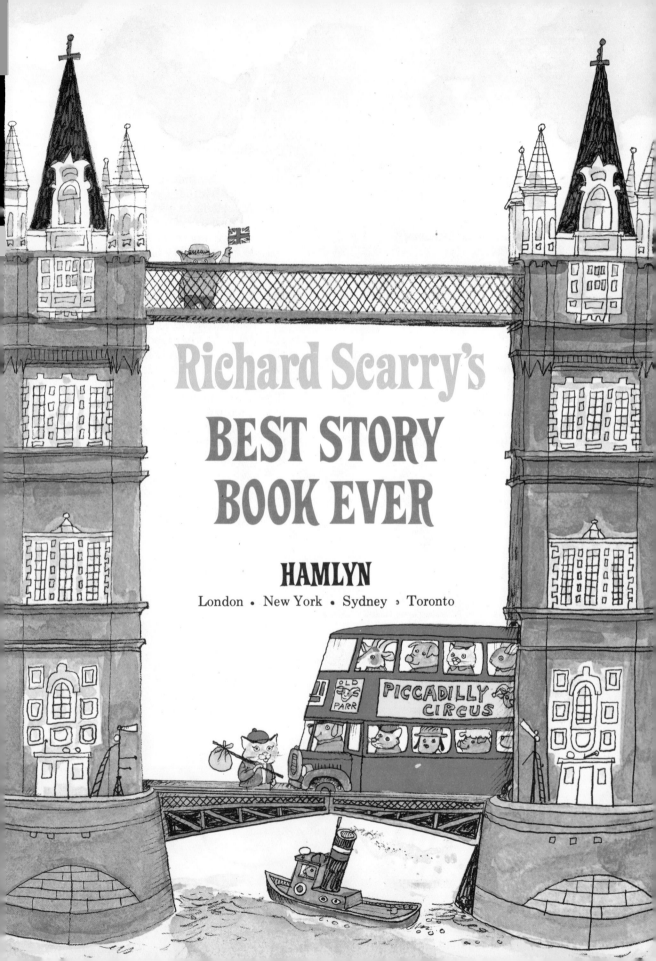

Richard Scarry's
BEST STORY BOOK EVER

HAMLYN

London · New York · Sydney · Toronto

Contents

First published 1970
Ninth impression 1977
Published by The Hamlyn Publishing Group Limited
London • New York • Sydney • Toronto
Astronaut House, Feltham, Middlesex, England
by arrangement with Western Publishing Company, Inc.
© Copyright 1968, 1967, 1966, 1965, 1964, 1963
1961, 1960, 1959, 1958, 1955, 1954, 1950 by Western
Publishing Company, Inc. 'The Storybook Dictionary'
© Copyright 1966 and 'The Golden Go-Go Library'
© Copyright 1977 by Richard Scarry
ISBN 0 601 08656 2
Printed in Czechoslovakia by Polygrafia, Prague
51014/9

window   curtains

THE NEW DAY

It is the morning of a new day.
The sun is shining.
Little Bear gets up out of bed.

First he washes
his face and hands.

Then he brushes
his teeth.

He combs
his hair.

He dresses
himself.

He makes
his bed.

He comes promptly when
he is called to breakfast.

Bear sits up straight in his chair.

He is very hungry. This is what he eats.

cold fruit juice

warm cereal

with cream

He doesn't eat the toaster.

pancakes

with butter and maple syrup

fried eggs

bacon

toast

honey

jam

hot cocoa

cool milk

and a waffle.

When he finishes eating breakfast he helps his mother to wash and dry the dishes.

cup

saucer

plate

bowl

fork

knife

spoon

glass

jar

pitcher

frying pan

lid

saucepan

dish

bottle

juice squeezer

Now he is ready to play with his friends.

THE RABBIT FAMILY'S HOUSE

Father Rabbit, Mother Rabbit,
and the Rabbit Brothers
are getting ready for the new day.
Their friend Owl is waiting
for the two brothers to come out
to play. Can you find him?

roof

chimney

father   mirror

lamp

bed

bedroom

cupboard   dining room

kitchen   table

sink

back door   chair   floor

stove

mother

woodpile   lawn   bird bath

sun

television aerial

WHOO

owl

smoke

light switch

television set

record player

hassock

bunk bed

bathroom

upstairs hall

boys' bedroom

front door

outside light

living room

picture

candle

telephone

fireplace

stairs

sofa or couch

lamp

front hall

door mat

rug

stone path

window

FEED BIG HILDA HIPPO HER ABC

Charlie Chipmunk has invited Big Hilda Hippo to dinner. But Charlie can't decide what to feed her. Will you help Charlie pick the proper ABC food to feed Big Hilda?

Aa

Would you feed her an **automobile**?
Or an **apple**?
Which would you feed her?

Bb

Would a **bed** be good to eat?
Or a **banana**?

Did you ever see a hippo eat a **bed**

Cc

Would she like to eat
a **clock**?
Or a **carrot**?

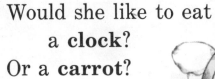

If she ate a **clock**
she might always say "Tick-tock."

Dd

Would you serve her
a **doughnut**
with a hole?

Or a **drum**?

Do you eat a **drum** with a fork
or with a spoon?

Ee

Do you think
she would
like an **egg**?
Or an **engine**?

Which would you prefer?

Ff

Is a **fan** good to eat?
Or **fudge**?

Gg

Would you give her **grapes**?
Or a **glove**?

If she ate one **glove** do you think
she should eat another so that
she would have a pair?

Hh

Would she like to eat a **hat**?
Or a **hot dog**?

Do you put mustard
on the **hats** you eat?

Ii

I know she would like some **ice cream**. Wouldn't you?

Jj

Do you think she would
like a juicy **jeep**?
Or **jam**?

What does a **jeep** taste like?
Does it taste like **jam**?

Kk

How would Hilda like a nice
ripe **kite**?

Or do you think a candy **kiss** is nicer?

Ll

Is Hilda hungry enough to
eat all this **laundry**?

Maybe she would like
some **lemonade** instead.

Mm

Shall we feed her
a **mop**?

Or a great big slice of **melon**?

Nn

Do you think she would like
to chew on a **nest**?

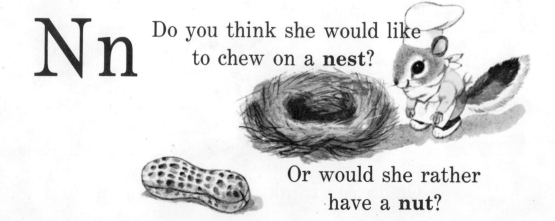

Or would she rather
have a **nut**?

Oo

Shall we feed her some nice fresh **overalls**?

Or an **orange**?

Pp

How about a nice **piano** to munch on?

Or a **peach**?

A **piano** is a lot more to eat than a **peach**. Wouldn't you rather eat a **piano**?

Qq

Do you eat a **quilt** while sitting up or lying down?

I don't think Hilda wants to eat a **quilt**.

Rr

Is Hilda hungry enough to eat a **refrigerator**?
Or would she prefer a **roast** of beef?

Ss

Now, shall we give her a
   sandwich with salt on it?
Or a **stove** with pepper on it?

16

Tt

Termites are little insects who like to eat **tables** and anything else made of wood. Would Hilda like to eat a **table** or a **tomato**?

Wow! Look at that termite eating that **table!**

Uu

Anyone who would try to eat an **umbrella** would be very silly. Please don't feed an **umbrella** to Hilda. It tastes awful.

V v   Instead, feed Hilda her **vitamins**.

W w

She will need a glass of **water** to wash them down.

X x

Hilda has finished her dinner.
She puts her knife and fork on her plate.
They look like the letter **X**.

Y y   She opens her mouth wide and **yawns**.

Zz

She is sleepy after such a big meal.
Off to sleep she goes. **ZZZzzzzzzzzzzzz!**

Hilda wants to thank you and Charlie for feeding her.
This is what she ate.

A B C D E F G

H I J K L M O

N

P Q R S T

U V W X Y Z

And if you are hungry tonight before
    you go to bed—eat something!
But . . . never, never, never
    eat your bed!

TOYS

tricycle

Toys and games have names, too.
When you play with toys,
it is more fun if you
share them with your friends.
When you play games you may win
and sometimes you may lose.
Bear is a good sport. He is
losing a game but he might
win the next time. Do you think
he might win the next game?

doll

blocks

teddy bear

rocking-horse

Bear is losing.

game

Rabbit is winning.

castle

croquet

toy soldiers

tea-set

robot

racing car

typewriter

bean bags

doll's house

scooter

glider

bow and arrow

WORDS TO LEARN

PARTS OF THE BODY

Everyone has a **body**.
Every **body** has many
different parts to it.
We use words to name parts
of the **body**. Ali Cat and
Squeaky have drawn pictures
which show us the different
parts. Some of us have tails.
What kind of tail do you have?

THE HEAD

hair
eye
ear
cheek
nose
face
tooth
tongue
lips
chin

THE BODY

head
wrist
neck
shoulder
elbow
chest
arm
stomach
paw or hand
waist
knee
claw or finger
foot
tail
leg
claw or toe
heel
ankle

mouth
teeth

TAILS

THE FAMILY

Grandma

Mother

Sister Kitty

Uncle Louie

Father Cat

Babykins

Brother Tom

Aunty and
all the cousins

Uncle and Aunty Cat and their children
visit the Cat **family**. Uncle Louie is
Mother Cat's brother. All belong
to the same **family**.

January	April	July	October
February	May	August	November
March	June	September	December

THE MONTHS OF THE YEAR

There are four seasons in the year.
They are spring, summer,
autumn, and winter.

Sunday
Monday
Tuesday
Wednesday
Thursday
Friday
Saturday

THE DAYS OF THE WEEK

Ali Cat is teaching Squeaky
about **days**. A **day** is one
daytime and one **nighttime**.
A **day** has a morning, a noon,
an afternoon, an evening,
and a night. There are seven
days in a week. Can you
write them, Squeaky?
Very good, Squeaky.

Mother Goose Rhymes

With letters we can make words.
With words we can make rhymes
 and stories.
Let us read some Mother Goose
 rhymes.

Old Mother Goose,
When she wanted to wander,
Would ride through the air
On a very fine gander.

Tom, Tom, the piper' son,
Stole a pig and away did run.
The pig was eat, and Tom
 was beat,
And Tom went crying
 down the street.

GINGERBREAD PIGS

This little pig went to market,

This little pig stayed at home,

This little pig had roast beef,

This little pig had none,

And this little pig cried, Wee-wee-wee-wee-wee,
I can't find my way home.

Now let us read some stories.

THE FISHING CAT

by Patricia Scarry

A cat went down to the sea to fish.
He wanted to catch a whale.

Did he catch a big, big whale?

No!
He caught
a big, big log.

Did he toss the log back into the sea?

No. The cat did not.
He took out his knife and he cut the log.
He cut it here and there.
Now why did the cat do that?

He did it to make a fine fishing boat.

So LOOK OUT all you whales!

I AM A BUNNY

by Ole Risom

I am a bunny.
My name is Nicholas.
I live in a hollow tree.

In the spring, I like to pick flowers.

In the summer,
I listen to the insects
buzzing and humming.

In the autumn,
I like to watch the leaves
falling from the trees.

And, when winter comes,
I watch the snow falling from the sky.

Then I curl up in my hollow tree
and dream about spring.

GOOD-NIGHT
LITTLE BEAR

by Patricia Scarry

It is time for Little Bear to go to bed.
Mother Bear closes the story book.
She gives Little Bear a good-night kiss.

Then over to
his big furry father
runs the little bear.
Wheee!

Father Bear swings his little one high up on
to his shoulders for a ride to bed.

"Duck your head," calls Mother Bear, just in time.
And into the snug little bedroom they go.

Squeak!

The tiny bed sighs as Father Bear sits down.

"Now, into bed with you," he says.

He waits for Little Bear to climb down.

But Little Bear doesn't move.

He sits up on his father's shoulders and grins.

Father Bear waits. He yawns a rumbly yawn.

Is Father Bear falling asleep?

No. Suddenly he opens his eyes again.

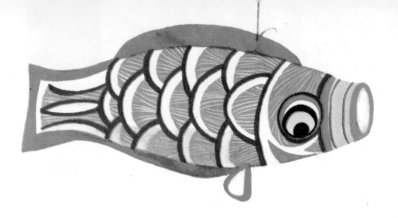

"Why, I must have been dreaming,"
says Father Bear, pretending to wake up.
But what's this?
There is no furry head on the pillow.

Where can Little Bear be?
Father Bear looks under the pillow.

Nobody there.
He doesn't seem to feel
something tickling his ear.

Aha!
There's a lump down under the blanket.
Father Bear pats the lump.
But it doesn't squeak or wiggle.
Can it be Little Bear?

Why, it's the toy teddy and the blue bunny
waiting for Little Bear to come to bed!

"Mother, that naughty bear is hiding,"
says Father Bear to Mother Bear, with a wink.
"Maybe he's hiding under the kitchen stove,"
says Mother Bear, who loves a joke.

Bang! Bang!
Father Bear rattles the pots and pans
on top of the stove.
"Little Bear, I'm coming to get you!" he roars.

Father Bear reaches under the stove.
He feels something soft and furry.
Is it Little Bear?

No.
It's only Father Bear's old winter mitten.

'Way up high Little Bear claps his paw
to his mouth. But not in time.
"I heard that Little Bear laugh," says Father.
"Now where can he be hiding?"

"Is he standing outside the front door?
I'll turn the knob softly—
and fling the door wide!"
No. There are no bears out there.
Just a family of fat little rabbits
nibbling lettuce in the garden.
"Shoo!" snorts Father Bear.

There's nobody up high, on the china shelf.
"Ouch!"
Little Bear bumps his head.
"Who said Ouch?" asks Father Bear.
"Mother, did you say Ouch?"
"Not I," smiles Mother Bear.
Oh, she is a tease.

"Now where is that naughty bear hiding?
He wouldn't run away.
Not a little bear who is always hungry
for chocolate cake."
And that big Daddy Bear cuts himself a huge piece
of chocolate cake right under the little bear's nose.

Little Bear suddenly feels hungry.
But just then Father Bear stops smack
in front of the mirror.
"Why, there he is," roars the big bear.
"But you couldn't find me," squeaks Little Bear,
reaching for chocolate cake.

Wheee!
Off Daddy's shoulders and down to the sofa.
Bounce. Bounce. Bounce.
"Wasn't that a good hiding-place, Mummy?
No one could find me up there."

"But I've found you now," says Father Bear.
Little Bear wiggles and giggles under his Daddy's
strong arm . . . all the way into bed.

"Did I really fool you, Daddy?"
asks Little Bear.
Father Bear just laughs and winks.
Do you think Father Bear knew all the time?

WORK MACHINES

Busy, busy, busy bears.
Most of the bears are busy
moving earth with their machines.

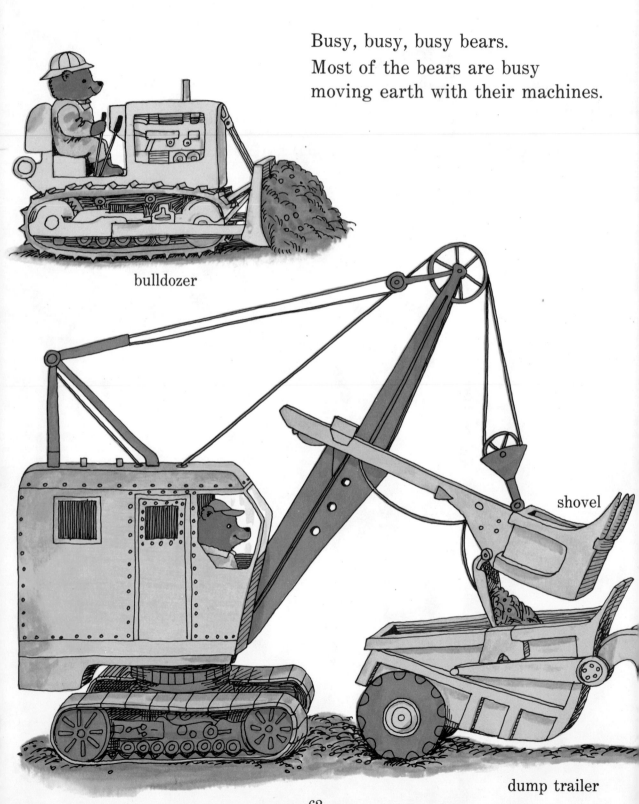

bulldozer

shovel

dump trailer

But there is one bear
who has a machine which
does something else to the earth.
Which one is it? What is he doing?

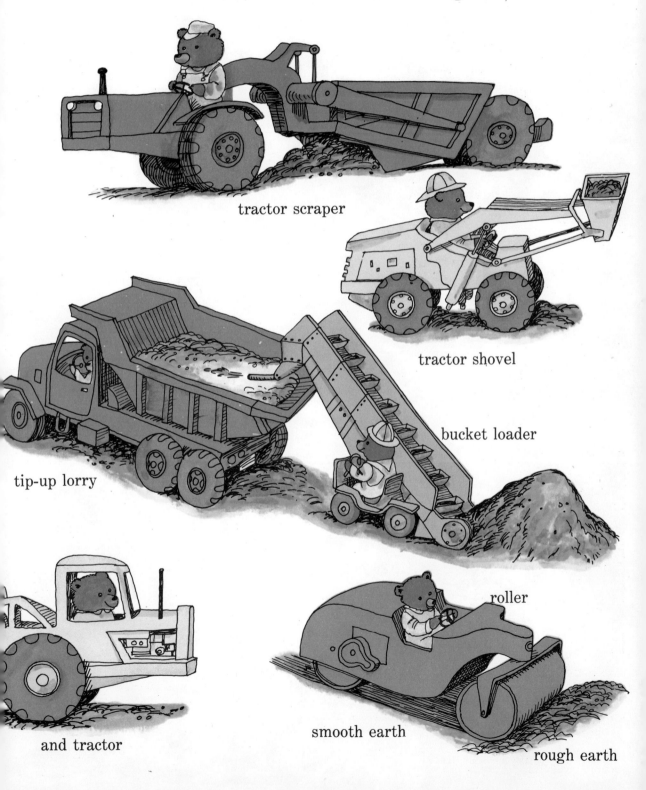

tractor scraper

tractor shovel

bucket loader

tip-up lorry

roller

and tractor

smooth earth

rough earth

ANIMALS

All **animals** move about.

bee

mouse

monkey

Some **animals** hop,
jump, and run.

kangaroo

pig

otter

grasshopper

crocodile

Some **animals**
have tails.

cat

tiger

squirrel

ant

anteater

Some **animals** have
big noses.

elephant

crab

turtle

mouse

Some have shells.

warthog

Dingo Dog

Some **animals** are beautiful.

Some drive too fast.

swordfish

tunafish

not really?

no fooling!

shark

Some **animals** tell stories.

pig

lion

walrus

Some eat too much.

Some help other **animals**
get well when they are sick.

stork

heron

rooster

penguin

hen and
chickens

cat

pig

All **animals** love
to read books.

Some **animals** hate to take baths.

The pretty coloured birds like
to have their picture taken.
Watch the birdie, birds!

birdie

kiwi

eagle

flamingo

parrot

duck

toucan

goose

puffin

turkey

chamois

gnu

reindeer

antelope

kudu

musk ox

yak

Some **animals** have horns.

bighorn
sheep

Some **animals** are insects.

Some insects dive.

Some insects wear four shoes.

praying mantis

cricket

beetle

bear

Some **animals** wear coats that are too big for them.

tiger

Some **animals** wiggle and crawl and spell words.

Some are not very good fishermen.

octopus

pig

Some **animals** can reach all the way across the table. My, what bad manners!

potato grub

worm

Some **animals** live in houses.

snake

At least one sleeps with his shoe on.

frog

The frogs are lucky to have a swimming pool.

double bass

triangle

trumpet

Some **animals** make very fine music.
Toot toot!
Boom boom!
Twang twang!

cymbals

THE CATS' MEOWERS

piano

drum

goat

cat

owl

mouse

moose

canoe

Some ride in boats.

Baron von Crow

Some **animals** ride on trains . . .

baboon

wolf

. . . while others
ride bicycles.

laughing hyena

71

owl

bird

Some **animals** fly.

Some insects fly.

skunk

All flies fly.
Close the door please!

raccoon

rabbit

leopard

Paper aeroplanes fly.
Some **animals**
are naughty.

Mr. Fixit Fox wears
rubber boots to keep
his feet dry.

leaking pipe

Grandma sews Tom Cat's trousers
to keep his seat warm.

SHARES

square

cone

oval

round

star

diamond

Shapes can be square, or round, or oval or triangular. Everything has a **shape**. Even Big Hilda Hippopotamus has a **shape**.

1, one
2, two
3, three
4, four
5, five
6, six
7, seven
8, eight
9, nine
10, ten

NUMBERS

Ali is teaching Squeaky about **numbers**. Now, repeat after Ali:

LINES

Ali Cat drew a curved **line**. Now he is drawing a straight **line**.

curved

straight

73

Farmer Pig

FARMER PIG PLANTED
A SEED OF CORN
IN THE GROUND.

THE RAIN CAME DOWN
AND WET THE SEED
THE SEED
STARTED TO GROW.

THE SUN
SHONE DOWN,
AND WARMED
THE SEED.
SOON,
LITTLE LEAVES
SPROUTED UP
FROM THE GROUND.

IT GREW AND GREW.

FINALLY,
IT HAD THREE EARS OF CORN,
READY TO BE PICKED.

FARMER PIG GAVE
ONE EAR TO MR. CROW.

HE GAVE ONE EAR TO HIS WIFE.
SHE LOVED CORN!

AND WITH HIS KNIFE,
FARMER PIG MADE
THE THIRD EAR
INTO A PIPE!
ISN'T IT WONDERFUL
TO THINK OF WHAT
YOU CAN DO WITH
ONE LITTLE SEED!

brook

meadow

haystacks

apple orchard

corn field

ploughed field

lane

fence

stone wall

vegetable garden

gate

barn

farmyard

hayloft

water pump

farmhouse

ON THE FARM

Farmer Hee Haw is
working on his farm.
He is growing vegetables
to sell at the market.
He doesn't have any time
to spend with visitors.

hoe

ladder

scythe

rake

milk can

pail

farm truck

tractor

pitchfork

trailer

Farmer Hee Haw is taking the vegetables to the market to sell. My! That is a bumpy road!

corn

peas

celery

asparagus

lettuce

potato

tomatoes

beetroots

onions

cauliflower

carrots

turnip

cucumbers

beans

pumpkin

cabbage

squash

MEALTIME

candlestick

bread basket

napkin

teaspoon

mug

knife

plate for a big pickle

cup and saucer

plate

fork

bowl

soup ladle

butter knife

glass

chair

soup tureen

tablespoon

soup spoon

pitcher

butter plate

tablecloth

Mealtime, Pickles Pig! Before you sit down, do what you should always do before you eat.

Good! Now that you have washed your face you may eat your pickle and your fruit.

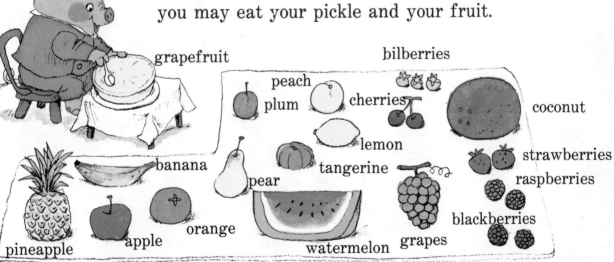

grapefruit

bilberries

peach

plum

cherries

coconut

lemon

banana

tangerine

strawberries

pear

raspberries

blackberries

pineapple

apple

orange

watermelon

grapes

Dear me! Pickles Pig ate too much. He was so sleepy he lay down and took a nap!

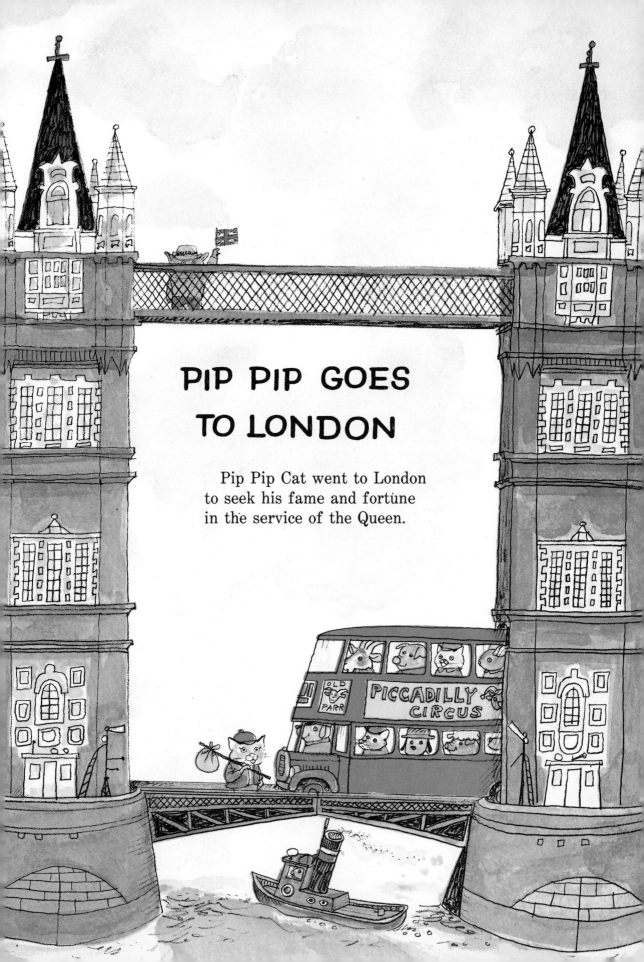

PIP PIP GOES TO LONDON

Pip Pip Cat went to London
to seek his fame and fortune
in the service of the Queen.

First, he went to
the Tower of London,
to see if he could be
a Beefeater,
which means a Guardian
of the Queen's jewels.
No! They didn't need
any more guards.

When he went
to the Queen's palace
the guard wouldn't
talk to him.
He was too busy
guarding the Queen.

At the Admiralty, where they guard
the Queen's Navy, he was afraid of
being stepped upon and so he quickly left.

Pip Pip was very sad. He wouldn't be able to serve
the Queen after all. "The Queen must be very sad too,"
he said to himself. "She has lost her ring."

He passed a fountain into
which people had thrown pennies
for good luck. He saw
something which didn't
look like a penny.
It was golden! It glittered!

It was a ring!
Maybe it was the Queen's ring!!
He showed it to a policeman.
    They hurried off to see
the Queen. It was the Queen's ring!
She was very happy to have it back.

    The Queen made Pip Pip
"The Queen's Guard of
Her Majesty's Fountains."
Every day, he scooped out
the "good luck" pennies.
    The Queen used the money
to buy food for the poor
stray cats who had no
homes and lived in alleys.
Wasn't she a nice Queen?

BUILDINGS

Ali Cat is drawing pictures
of different kinds of **buildings**.
Squeaky is colouring the pictures.

windmill

palace

cottage

half-timbered
house

barn

castle

apartment
houses

chalet

brick house

factory

tower

lighthouse

Can you draw a picture of the **building** you live in?

A Tale of Tails

WILLY PIG
DID NOT LIKE HIS TAIL.
HE THOUGHT HE WOULD
BE HAPPY IF ONLY HE
HAD A TAIL LIKE A FOX.

No! A FOX TAIL
IS TOO BUSHY FOR A PIG.

IF ONLY HE HAD
A TAIL LIKE A COW.

No! A COW'S TAIL
IS TOO LONG FOR A PIG.

MAYBE IF HE HAD
A BEAUTIFUL GREEN
ALLIGATOR TAIL?

NO! NO! NO!
AN ALLIGATOR'S TAIL
LOOKS SILLY ON A PIG!
WILLY PIG DECIDED THAT
A PIG'S CURLY TAIL
IS THE BEST TAIL,
FOR A PIG.

DON'T YOU THINK SO?

WHAT ANIMALS DO

The rooster struts.

The duck waddles.

The goose waggles.

The ant
crawls.

The bear shuffles.

The mother kangaroo hops.

The baby kangaroo rides.

The frog leaps.
The fly flies.

And little chicks come
peep-peeping out of their eggs.

More Mother Goose Rhymes

Two little dicky birds,
Sitting on a wall;
One named Peter,
The other named Paul.
Fly away, Peter!
Fly away, Paul!
Come back, Peter!
Come back, Paul!

Little Miss Muffet
Sat on a tuffet,
Eating her curds and whey;
There came a big spider,
Who sat down beside her
And frightened Miss Muffet away.

London Bridge is falling down,
Falling down, falling down,
London Bridge is falling down,
My fair lady.

MR. HEDGEHOG'S
CHRISTMAS PRESENT

by Kathryn Jackson

London town was even more wonderful than
Mr. Hedgehog had imagined. The shops were
a miracle of shining lights and finery.

Even the mice went about with presents for their friends, and "Merry Christmas" on their lips. "I should like to get a present for Mrs. Hedgehog!" said Mr. Hedgehog to himself.

What should it be?

Not a fur coat. Mrs. Hedgehog had one that suited her perfectly.

Not a diamond tiara. That would be too heavy for her head. Might make it ache!

Surely not a bottle of scent. Hedgehogs like the smell of fern and hawthorn.

Suddenly something lovely caught Mr. Hedgehog's eye. A bright red apple lay in the clean snow near the kerb, lost and forgotten.

Mr. Hedgehog picked it up and brushed off the snow. He polished it with his mittens. Solemnly he offered it to his wife, and said,

"A Merry Christmas, my dear!"

Mrs. Hedgehog kissed him. "Thank you," she said. "I'll make us a big, sweet, warm apple pie!"

The little Hedgehogs, one and all, smacked their lips and shouted "Merry Christmas!"

And arm in arm the Hedgehog family hurried home to their cosy burrow, which soon smelled excitingly of apple and spice and crisp pastry browning—the very merriest kind of Christmas smell!

WHISPER
IN MY EAR

One day Elephant went
to visit Mrs. Mouse.
"I am too big to come
inside your house,"
he said. "Please tell me
what you have inside it."

"First you must be
very quiet," she said.
"Then if you will lift me
up with your trunk, I will
whisper in your ear."

1 one

"I have **one** handsome husband
inside my house," said Mrs. Mouse.
"He is helping me do the housework."

one

One handsome husband.
Is he helping with the housework?

2 two

"In my kitchen I have **two** pots.
In one pot I cook meat and in
the other pot I cook vegetables."
"It smells delicious," said Elephant.

one

two

Here are her two pots cooking meat and vegetables.
Mr. Mouse is tasting to see if the vegetables are done.

3 three

"How many beds do you have in your house?" asked Elephant.
"I have **three** beds,"
said Mrs. Mouse in a whisper.

one

two

three

Mr. Mouse likes to make his own bed.

4 four

"I have **four** clocks that tell the time.
"My favourite one is the cuckoo clock."

Sometimes it frightens Mr. Mouse.

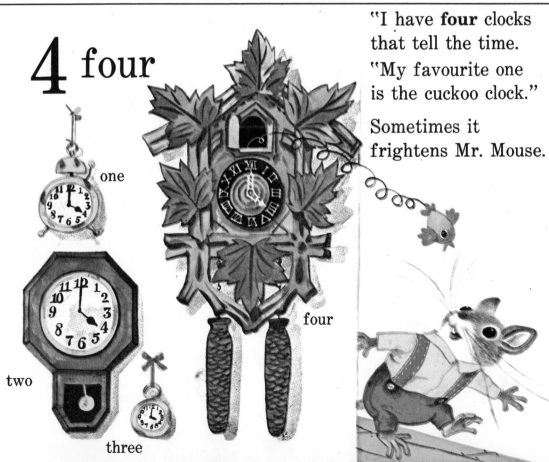

one

two

three

four

5 five

"In the evening when it gets dark, **five** lamps make my little house light and cheery," she said.

one

two

three

four

five

Mr. Mouse is very good at dusting the five lamps.

6 six

"In my house I have **six** chairs," whispered Mrs. Mouse. "Some are hard and some are soft."

one

two

three

four

five

six

Mr. Mouse likes to sit in a soft chair.

7 seven

"I have **seven** pretty hats," she whispered in Elephant's ear.

Mr. Mouse is trying on one of her hats.

---

8 eight

"I am a very neat housewife. I have **eight** brooms to help me keep the house clean," she whispered.

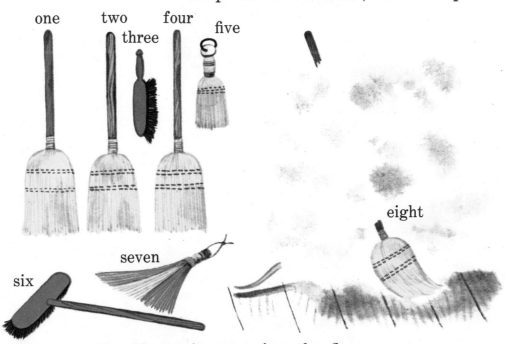

Mr. Mouse is sweeping the floor.

9 nine

"To make my house look pretty, I have **nine** plants which I water every day."

one

two

three

four

five

six

seven

eight

nine

Oh, dear! Mrs. Mouse forgot to water one of her nine plants today.

10 ten

"I have **ten** books which I like to read,"
she whispered to Elephant.
"What are the names of your books?" asked Elephant.

one

two

three

four

five

six

seven

eight

nine

ten

Mr. Mouse likes to read books, too.
What is he reading about?

11 eleven

"I have **eleven** beautiful pictures hanging on my wall," she whispered.

one
two
three
four
five
six
seven
eight
nine
ten
eleven

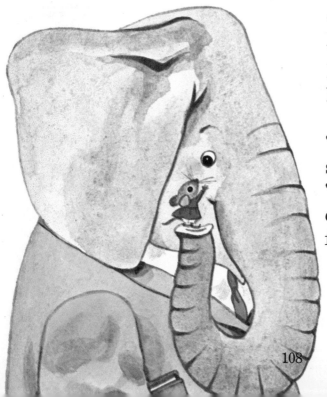

"You certainly have a very nice house," said Elephant. "But why do you have to whisper in my ear?"

"Oh, I have to whisper," said Mrs. Mouse in a whisper, "because I have **twelve** darling children who are fast asleep in the bedroom."

12 twelve

Can you count **twelve** children taking their naps?
Why don't you whisper in Mrs. Mouse's ear and
tell her that the children have finished
their naps and want to go out to play?

THANK YOU!

A CASTLE IN DENMARK

Here are some rules that you must obey if you live in a castle; or even if you live in a house.

Behave yourself at the dinner table.

Don't run in your castle or house.

Don't lean out of windows. You might fall out.

When they meet the King and Queen, boys should bow and girls should curtsy.

Wipe your muddy feet before you enter the castle.

Do not fish in the moat.

Feed the dragon when he is hungry.

Don't be naughty. Naughty people must sit in the dungeon.

Keep a light burning, so that the witches who live in your castle can find their way home at night.

Be careful where you fly your kite.

Don't land your helicopter on the roof.

All ghosts must put their sheets in the washing machine when they get dirty.

All witches must put their brooms away when they have finished with them.

⋯ep your suit of armour well ⋯ed so that you won't squeak.

Don't leave things on the stairs where people can trip over them.

Don't shoot the cannons without permission.

Don't climb inside cannons unless you are a cannonball.

⋯on't let down the ⋯rawbridge to strangers.

If you are coming to visit make sure the drawbridge is down before you try to cross it.

CARS AND LORRIES

taxi

racing car

breakdown lorry

police car

ambulance

mail van

fire engine

estate car

delivery van

refuse lorry

Dingo has a new car,
a shiny red racing car.
Look out, all you other cars.
Look out, lorries and buses and fire engines.

jeep

wind-screen
headlight
tail-light
bumper
wheel
steering-wheel
tyre

lorry

bus

motorcycle

motor scooter

policeman

traffic light

tip-up lorry

sports car

saloon car

double decker bus

direction sign

Oh that Dingo! He is very naughty
to be such a nuisance, isn't he?
Ali Cat is quietly painting a poster.
Can you read the words on the poster?

More Cars and Lorries

A taxi will take us anywhere we want to go in a hurry.

The oldtime "tin lizzie" was loved by many people. It was the most popular car of its day.

The police car patrols the streets to help keep us all safe.

The fire chief's car whizzes by on the way to a fire.

The estate car used to look like this. Part of it was made of sturdy, polished wood.

A sports car is smaller than most cars and can go very fast.

The breakdown lorry tows the wrecked car to the garage to be repaired.

The sturdy jeep can go places other cars can't go, up hill or down hill or in mud or sand.

The back part of the tip-up lorry tips up and dumps its load.

PETROL

The petrol tanker brings petrol to the garage.

A racing car is very high powered and goes very fast. Its engine makes a loud roar.

The happy little nursery-school bus takes children to and from their nursery school.

Sooner or later most cars end up like this.

MOTHER GOOSE NURSERY SCHOOL

THE FOX AND
THE CROW

Told by Patricia Scarry

A crow sat in a high tree holding a tasty bit of cheese in her mouth.

Along came a hungry wart hog.

"The crow will laugh when she sees my funny face," he said. "And when she laughs, she'll drop the cheese."

He called to the crow, making a funny face.

But she didn't even smile.

Along came a hungry little elephant.

"Drop the cheese to me, Crow," said the elephant, "or I will give you a shower bath!"

But the crow did not drop the cheese, even though WHOOSH! the elephant's trunk sent up a stream of water.

"Drop the cheese to me," called the big brown bear, "and you may have this pot of honey."

But the crow did not like honey, and she did not drop the cheese.

The crow was about to eat the cheese when along came a cunning little fox.

"Oh beautiful crow," he called, "you are lovely to see. A bird with such charming feathers must sing a pretty tune. Please sing for me."

Now the crow had never been told she was pretty, although she thought she was. And she had never been told that her voice was pretty.

She opened her beak and rasped an ugly CAAW!

Down tumbled the cheese, into the fox's mouth!

Now wasn't she a silly bird to let that sweet talk fool her?

More
Mother Goose
Rhymes

There was an old woman tossed up in a basket,
Seventeen times as high as the moon;
Where she was going I couldn't but ask it,
For under her arm she carried a broom.
Old woman, old woman, old woman, said I,
Where are you going to up so high?
To sweep the cobwebs out of the sky,
And I'll be with you by-and-by.

WHEN YOU GROW UP

What would you like to be
when you are grown up?
Would you like to be
a good cook like your father?
Or would you like to be
a doctor or a nurse?
What would you like to be?

policeman

fireman

nurse   milkman

farmer

cowboy

carpenter   musician

dentist

secretary

good cook

singer

artist

pilot

driver

teacher

ticket inspector

traveller

shopkeeper

dancer

daddy

mummy

COUSCOUS,
THE ALGERIAN DETECTIVE

Couscous was the best detective in Algiers. He was very good at disguising himself to look like someone else.

Couscous was in disguise as he walked past the robber's den of Pepe le Gangstair. He was trying to think of a way to get inside the robber's den and capture Pepe and his band of dirty rats.

Can you tell which one is Couscous? No! You can't—because Couscous is so good at disguising himself!

Suddenly Couscous had a good idea. He hurried back to the police station, where his cat and mouse assistants were waiting. He took off his disguise and told them of his plan.

"You have a very clever plan, Couscous!" they all agreed.

That night when it was dark, a small group came
to the door of the robber's den and knocked.
Knock! Knock! Knock!

"Who is knocking at my door?" growled Pepe le Gangstair.

"It is I, the pretty dancing girl Fatima, with my troupe of musicians," a soft sweet voice answered. "We have come to entertain you."

"Come in, come in," said Pepe. He opened the door and let them in.
Oh, how beautifully Fatima danced! She was magnificent!

"MORE! MORE!" shouted Pepe.

"I have more for you," said Fatima, "but first I must blindfold you, as I have a big surprise."

So she blindfolded Pepe and the robbers and led them out of the door. . . .

. . . into the police wagon!

The robbers were prisoners! They had been captured by that clever master of disguise COUSCOUS!!!

My! That Couscous is a clever fellow.

Tom, the Fishing Cat

TOM CAT WENT FISHING.

HE CAUGHT A LITTLE FISH!

HE CAUGHT A BIGGER FISH!

LOOK! THERE IS A GREAT BIG ONE!

LOOK OUT, TOM!

NOW WHO WAS CAUGHT?

130

Count with Hooty Owl

HOOTY OWL AND HIS MOTHER WENT TO THE STORE AND BOUGHT ONE PIECE OF CHEESE

THEY BOUGHT TWO ORANGES

AND THREE APPLES.

MOTHER OWL PICKED OUT FOUR WHITE EGGS.

WHAT COULD BE NICER FOR SUPPER THAN FIVE ONIONS?

SIX PICKLES, MAYBE?

THEY BOUGHT SEVEN FAT HOT DOGS FROM THE BUTCHER.

AND THEN, HOME THEY WENT FOR SUPPER.

SEVEN
SIX
FIVE
FOUR
THREE
TWO
ONE....? "WHAT BECAME OF THAT ONE PIECE OF CHEESE?" ASKED MOTHER, WITH A SMILE. I THINK SHE KNEW. DON'T YOU?

More Mother Goose Rhymes

Elsie Marley is grown so fine,
She won't get up to feed the swine,
But lies in bed till eight or nine,
Lazy Elsie Marley.

THE HUNGRY BEGGARS

The beggars smelled something cooking in
Mamma Bear's kitchen. Mamma Bear had baked a cake.

Mamma Bear told them she would give them each a piece
if they would mind the house while she went shopping.
My! That is hard cake, Mamma!

Mamma returning home.

refrigerator

cuckoo clock

spice cabinet

teapot

counter

dishwasher

freezer

mop and pail

washing machine

sink

frying pan

a cook beating

saucepan

lid

bun tin

roasting pan

soup ladle

egg beater

spilled ketchup

potato peeler

cake ring

cook book

mixing bowl

funnel

mustard jar

jug

The beggars decided to make a soft cake while Mamma was out. They were going to surprise her with it when she returned.

Mamma surprised the beggars. She made them go to work and clean up the mess they had made.

135

IN THE FLOWER GARDEN

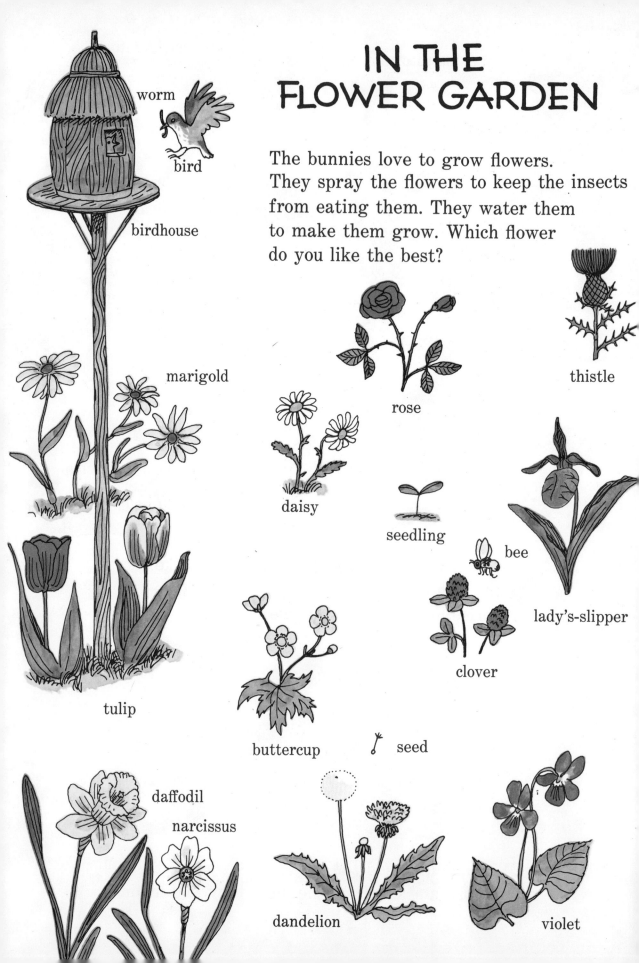

worm

bird

birdhouse

The bunnies love to grow flowers. They spray the flowers to keep the insects from eating them. They water them to make them grow. Which flower do you like the best?

marigold

rose

thistle

daisy

seedling

bee

lady's-slipper

clover

tulip

buttercup

seed

daffodil

narcissus

dandelion

violet

morning-glory

zinnia

hollyhock

foxglove

speedwell

pink

aster

insect-spray can

American bluebell

sweet William

petunia

pansy

beetle

flower basket

watering can

trowel

fork

lily of the valley

flower pot

137

Police Officer Montey is everyone's friend. He is very smart. He says:

"Cross the road at the crossing."
"Always look both ways to see that no cars are coming."
"Don't run! Always walk!"

OFFICER MONTEY OF MONACO

"Never throw anything at someone. You might hurt him."

"Never push or hit anyone. No one likes a bully."

"Never, never play where there is deep water. There might not be anyone around to pull you out!"

DANGER

"Never lean out of a car window."

"Never chase a ball into the road."

"Play on the pavement or in your garden. Never play in the road."

"Never go anywhere with someone you don't know."

"Behave yourself and act like a little lady or gentleman when you are in a car."

"And whatever you do, don't bring home stray alligators! They might bite!"

139

IS THIS THE HOUSE
OF MISTRESS MOUSE?

This is the house
of Mister Mouse.
He lived all alone
and he was very lonely.
One day he received a
letter from Mistress Mouse.
The letter said:
"Dear Mister Mouse,
I am very lonely too.
Will you please come
and visit me?
Love and kisses,
Mistress Mouse."

Mister Mouse said to himself,
"I would like very much to visit Mistress Mouse but I don't know where she lives.
"However, I will just have to get into my little car and go and look for her."

"There is a house just ahead,"
said Mister Mouse. "Perhaps that is
where Mistress Mouse lives."

He knocked on the door.

"Is this the house of Mistress Mouse?" he asked.

Mister Mouse was very frightened for that was the house of . . .

"MEOWWWRRR!"

. . . the house of
Mister **CAT!**

"What a cute little
mouse," thought
Mister Cat as he
watched him speed
away in his car.
"I wonder why he
was so frightened?"
But Mister Mouse
knew better than
to go into Mister
Cat's house. Didn't he?

Soon he came to a bright red barn.
He knocked on the barn door. It was
the house of . . .

"CUT-CUT-CUT-CU-DAHCUT"

. . . it was the house of Mrs. HEN and her baby chicks.

"Please don't bother me. I am teaching my chicks to scratch," she said.

And so Mister Mouse travelled on until he
came to a big, white castle. He knocked on the
castle door.

It was the castle of . . .

"ROARRRRR !!!"

...the castle of Mister

LION!!

He was in a very bad temper because he had a very bad toothache. Mister Mouse raced away as fast as he could go!

Finally he came to a cute little house in a lovely country lane.

He knocked on the pretty little yellow door.

"Is this the house of Mistress Mouse?" he asked.

The door slowly opened.

Sure enough! It WAS the house of
Mistress Mouse!

Mistress Mouse was so happy to see him.
And Mister Mouse was so happy to see her.

"Will you marry me so that we will never
again be lonely?" asked Mister Mouse.

"Why, YES! " said Mistress Mouse.

And so they were married by Father Mole.
Mister Mouse gave Mistress Mouse a golden
wedding ring with a bright diamond on top.

And from that day on
they were never lonely.

They went on picnics.

They took rides
in the country.

They went rowing
on the lake.

And then one night, after they had finished
their supper, they heard something.

It was a tiny "Squeak, squeak, squeak,"
coming from the bedroom.

What do you suppose it was that was
squeaking?

It was their BABY!

He wanted to be kissed good night.

"Good night, Daddy Mouse."

"Good night, Mummy Mouse."

"Good night, Baby Mouse."

"Good night."

COLOURS

This colour is yellow.

Baby chicks are yellow.
Daffodils are yellow, too.

This colour is blue.

Bunny's sailor
suit is blue.

The sky is blue.

This colour is red.

An apple is red.

This tricycle is red.

Blue and yellow make green.

A fat frog is green.

In summer,
leaves are green.

Red and yellow make orange.

Bunny's carrot
is orange.

A pumpkin is orange, too.

Blue and red make purple.

Violets and pansies are purple.

Grapes and plums are purple.

This colour is brown.

Red   Yellow   Blue   Black

make brown.

Puppy's fur is brown.

This little pony
is brown, too.

Red and white
make pink.

Roses and
bunny noses are pink.

Baby pigs are pink.

A snowman is white, and so is a duck.

This is black.

Sleepy bear cubs are black.

Red, yellow, blue, green—
a parrot has many colours.

Which is your favourite colour?

CLOTHES

Wiggles' clothes are scattered all about. Wiggles is looking for his other mitten. It's right where you put it, Wiggles.

mittens

pyjamas

slippers

vest

underwear

cap

shirt

swimming trunks

overalls

tie

hat

sneakers

gloves

jacket

muffler

rain hat

boots

raincoat

rubbers

shoes

belt

handkerchief

stocking cap

Why can't you hang up your clothes neatly the way your sister does?

stockings blouse

skirt

slip

panties

pinafore

nightgown

173

More Mother Goose Rhymes

Charley, Charley,
Stole the barley
Out of the baker's shop.
The baker came out
And gave him a clout,
Which made poor Charley hop.

Little Boy Blue,
Come blow your horn,
The sheep's in the meadow,
The cow's in the corn;
But where is the little boy
Tending the sheep?
He's under a haystack,
Fast asleep.
Will you wake him?
No, not I,
For if I do,
He's sure to cry.

One misty, moisty morning,
When cloudy was the weather,
There I met an old man
Clothed all in leather;
Clothed all in leather,
With cap under his chin.
How do you do, and how do you do,
And how do you do again?

AT THE AIRPORT

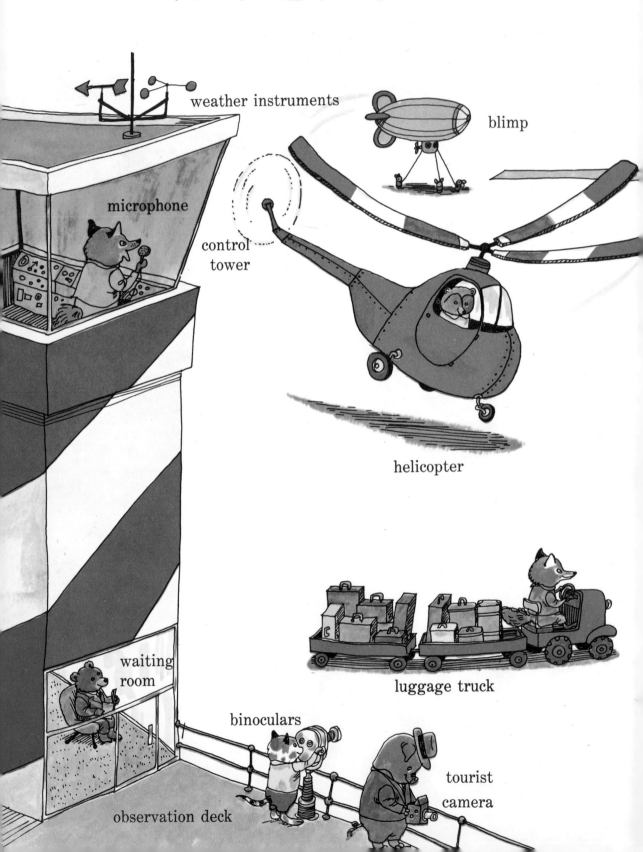

weather instruments

blimp

microphone

control tower

helicopter

waiting room

luggage truck

binoculars

tourist camera

observation deck

The man in the control tower is talking
into his microphone. He is talking to the
handsome pilot by radio. He is telling him
that he will have nice weather on his flight.

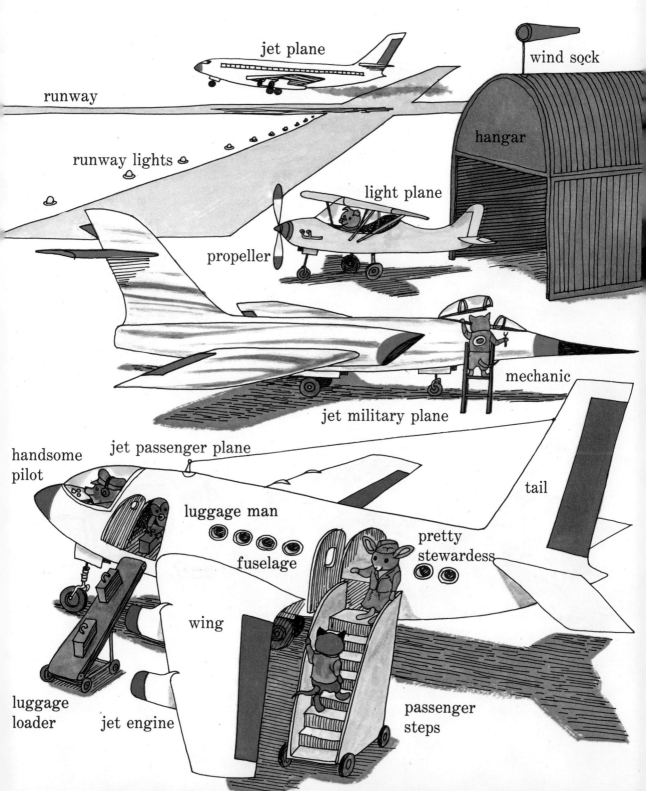

jet plane

wind sock

runway

hangar

runway lights

light plane

propeller

mechanic

jet military plane

jet passenger plane

handsome
pilot

tail

luggage man

pretty
stewardess

fuselage

wing

luggage
loader

jet engine

passenger
steps

Aeroplanes

THE FIRST AEROPLANES

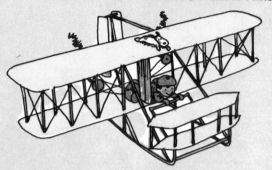

The very first heavier-than-air machine that would really fly was built by the Wright Brothers at Kitty Hawk, North Carolina.

Henri Farman, in France, flew his little biplane a distance of one mile. It was one of the first city-to-city flights.

The first important flight over water was made by Louis Blériot, a Frenchman. He flew across the English Channel.

The first light plane built in Europe was the tiny *"Demoiselle."*

A few years after the Wright Brothers' famous flight, Glenn Curtiss built successful aeroplanes.

The flimsy little *"Vin Fizz Flyer"* made the first flight across the United States.

WORLD WAR I FIGHTER PLANES

The black crosses painted on this Fokker monoplane show that it was German.

The Fokker triplane had three sets of wings.

The Spad was flown by American pilots.

The Albatros was the prize of German fighter squadrons.

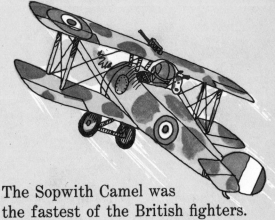

The Voisin was a French observation plane.

The Sopwith Camel was the fastest of the British fighters.

WORLD WAR II FIGHTER PLANES

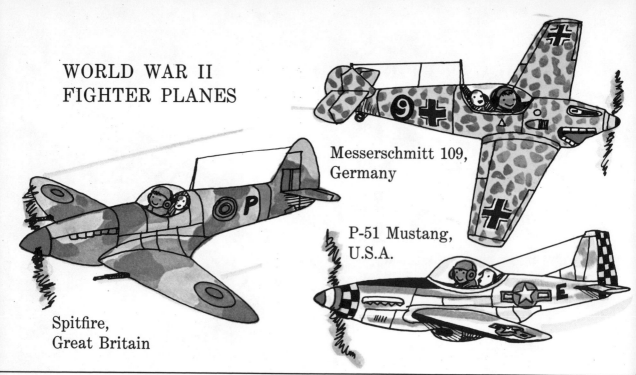

Messerschmitt 109, Germany

P-51 Mustang, U.S.A.

Spitfire, Great Britain

JET PLANES

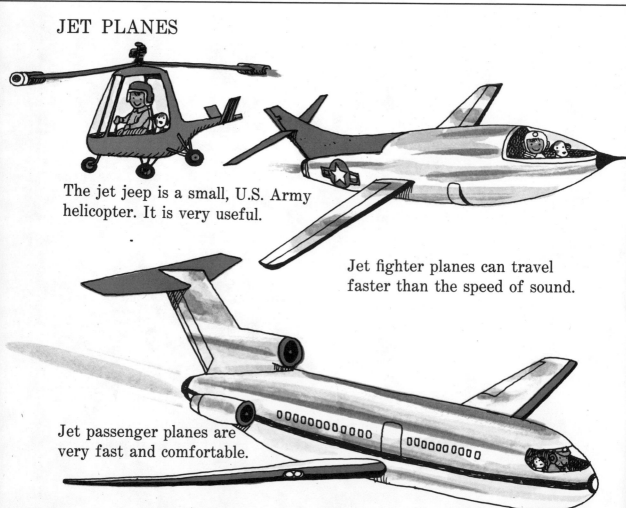

The jet jeep is a small, U.S. Army helicopter. It is very useful.

Jet fighter planes can travel faster than the speed of sound.

Jet passenger planes are very fast and comfortable.

Harry's Aeroplane Ride

HARRY CLIMBED
INTO HIS AEROPLANE

UP, UP, UP,
INTO THE SKY HE FLEW.

BUT
SOMETHING WAS WRONG!

GOOD GRACIOUS!
HE WAS FALLING
STRAIGHT DOWN!

MRS. PIG WAS HANGING
HER LAUNDRY OUT TO DRY.

HARRY WAS SAVED
BY MRS. PIG'S PANTIES!
HE IS LUCKY, ISN'T HE?

PIERRE,
THE PARIS POLICEMAN

Pierre was directing traffic when
suddenly he heard someone shout,
"Stop that robber! Stop that robber!"
A robber had stolen some jewels from
a shop. The robber ran to his car.

Pierre hopped on his bicycle and chased
after the robber. He blew his whistle
furiously. Brrrrrreeeeeeeeeet!

Through the crowded streets they raced.

AVENUE DES VOLEURS

Restaurant ☆☆☆
QUATRE ÉTOIL

Suddenly
the robber's
car crashed into a
pavement cafe. The robber
ran into the restaurant.
Brrrrrrrrrreeeeeeeeeet!

Pierre followed him.
Brrrrrrrrrreeeeeeeeeet. . . .

. . . into the kitchen.
  "Where is the robber?"
he roared at the chef.
The chef hadn't seen any robber.

Poor Pierre! He had lost
the robber.
  "Mmmmmmm, that soup
you are cooking smells good,"
said Pierre. "May I taste it?"

He put in his paw.
Look at what he found!
The robber! The robber
had hidden in the soup.
   Before Pierre took
the robber away
to be punished, they
all had some soup.

"This is the best
soup ever!" said the chef
to the robber.
"Perhaps after you
have been punished for
stealing, you will come back
and help me make soup
all the time? We will call
it 'Robber Soup.'"
   Everyone thought that
that was a good idea.

More Mother Goose Rhymes

Three little kittens,
They lost their mittens,
And they began to cry,
Oh, mother dear, we sadly fear
Our mittens we have lost.
What! lost your mittens,
You naughty kittens!
Then you shall have no pie.

The three little kittens,
They found their mittens,
And they began to cry,
Oh, mother dear, see here, see here,
Our mittens we have found.
Put on your mittens, You silly kittens,
And you shall have some pie.

The three little kittens
Put on their mittens,
And soon ate up the pie;
Oh, mother dear, we greatly fear
Our mittens we have soiled.
What! soiled your mittens,
You naughty kittens!
Then they began to sigh.

The three little kittens,
They washed their mittens,
And hung them out to dry;
Oh! mother dear, do you not hear
Our mittens we have washed?
What! washed your mittens,
Then you're good kittens.
But I smell a rat close by.

A NICE SURPRISE

If I write a letter

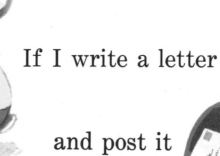

and post it

to someone I love,

someone I love may write a letter to me.

POLITE ELEPHANT

Everyone likes the polite elephant.
He knows the right things to say and do.
   When the polite elephant waits for the bus,
he takes his place in line. He never pushes
or shoves.

Sometimes
the bus
is crowded.

Sometimes the polite elephant goes visiting.
When someone comes
to the door, he takes off
his hat and says,
"Hello, Mrs. Smith.

How are you?"

The polite elephant always offers his seat to a lady.

The polite elephant is a good guest. He knows that some rooms are for sitting . . . and others are for playing.

When it's time for
the polite elephant
to go home,
he remembers
to thank his friends.
"Thank you,"
he says. "I've had
a nice time."

The polite elephant
is polite at home,
too. He always washes
his hands and face
before sitting at
the table.

He sits straight in his chair. When he wants something, he says, "Please." When he gets it, he says, "Thank you."

Sometimes the polite elephant's friends come to his house. He greets them at the door. "Hello," he says. "Please come in."

He introduces them
to his mother, "Mummy,
this is Jimmy."

The polite elephant is a good playmate.
He shares his toys with
his friends. And he is
very careful when he plays
with someone else's toys.

When his friends leave, the polite elephant goes to the door with them.

"Thank you for coming," he says.

If you should ever meet the polite elephant, he'll be just as polite to you. He'll tip his hat and say, "How do you do?"

CHIPMUNK'S
BIRTHDAY
PARTY

It was Chipmunk's birthday.

He invited his friends to come to his birthday party.

When they came he said,

"Hi, Rabbit! Hi, Mouse!
Hi, Goat! Hi, Donkey!
Hi, Frogs!"

"Now just a minute," said Mummy Chipmunk. "There'll be no birthday party until your ears are clean!"

Bunny Rabbit has big ears to clean, hasn't he?

Chipmunk and Mouse helped Mummy in the kitchen. Mummies always have to work hard when they give birthday parties.

MOUSE! What are you doing? Can't you wait until the party begins?

All the children went outside to play.

Chipmunk went sailing on the pond with Rabbit. They wore life jackets. They wanted to be safe just in case they should fall overboard.

Chipmunk chased butterflies with his net.
He was not a very good butterfly chaser.

Then they all played leapfrog.

Hide-and-seek was the next game.
Chipmunk was "it."
He tried to find his friends.
Can you find Mouse?
Where is he hiding?

It was time to stop playing games.

It was time to eat ice cream and drink lemonade. They put on funny hats. Froggie played his oboe.

Mouse picked some flowers.

He gave them to Mummy Chipmunk to
thank her for the birthday party. What a nice
Mouse! Do you have nice birthday parties, too?

THE BUNNY BOOK

by Patricia Scarry

The Daddy Bunny tossed his baby in the air.

"What will our baby be when he grows up?" asked the Daddy Bunny.

Baby Bunny sat in his basket and smiled at his bunny family. He knew what he would be.

"Maybe he will be a nice little postman who will bring a letter to every house and make the neighbours happy," said Daddy Bunny.

A hungry little bunny cousin wished that the baby would have a sweet shop.

"He could make lollypops with funny faces and give them to all the good children," wished the hungry little bunny cousin.

Great Uncle Bunny wanted the baby to be an engine driver on a big train.

"He would ring the bell when he was ready to start the train. And blow his horn, Toot! Toot! in the tunnels," said Great Uncle Bunny.

But the baby bunny did not want to be a postman or a shopkeeper or an engine driver on a big train when he grew up. He nibbled a carrot and looked wise. He knew what he wanted to be.

"I think our baby bunny should be an aeroplane pilot," said the little bunny sister. "What fun to jump out of his plane in a parachute!"

"Maybe he will be a fireman," said Great Aunt Bunny. "He could drive a fire engine to all the fires."

"He may grow up to be a farmer with a fine red tractor," said Uncle Bunny.

But the baby bunny did not want to be a
fireman or an aeroplane pilot or a farmer with
a fine red tractor when he grew up.
He bounced on his daddy's knee and laughed.
Can you guess what he will be?

He will have lots of little bunny children to feed when they are hungry. He will read them a story when they are sleepy, and tuck them into bed at night.

And that is what the baby bunny will grow up to be. A daddy rabbit.

More Mother Goose Rhymes

There was a crow sat on a stone,
When he was gone,
Then there was none.

Here am I,
Little jumping Joan;
When nobody's with me
I'm all alone.

There was an old crow
Sat upon a clod:
That's the end of my song,
That's odd.

Baa, baa, black sheep,
Have you any wool?
Yes, sir, yes, sir,
Three bags full;
One for my master,
And one for my dame,
And one for the little boy
Who lives down the lane.

Diddle, diddle, dumpling, my son John,
Went to bed with his trousers on;
One shoe off, and one shoe on;
Diddle, diddle, dumpling, my son John.

Jack, be nimble,
Jack, be quick,
Jack, jump over
The candlestick.

To market, to market, to buy a fat pig,
Home again, home again, jiggety-jig;
To market, to market, to buy a fat hog,
Home again, home again, jiggety-jog.

As I went to Bonner,
I met a pig
Without a wig,
Upon my word and honour.

Hey diddle, diddle,
The cat and the fiddle,
The cow jumped over the moon;
The little dog laughed
To see such sport,
And the dish ran away with the spoon.

Boats

Christopher Columbus sailed
to America in the year 1492
on the "*Santa Maria.*"

The Pilgrims sailed to America
on the "*Mayflower.*"

Pirates used to sail the seas
in search of treasure ships.

Many sailors like to row a little rowing-boat.

An outboard motorboat speeds over the waves.

A sport fishing boat is used for deep-sea fishing.

The racing boat skims the top of the water.

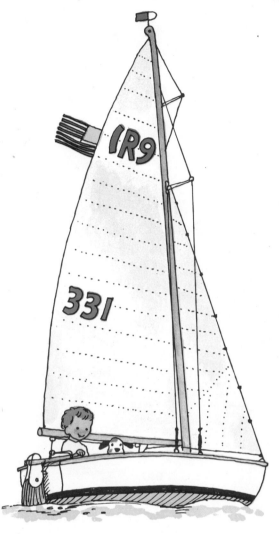

Wind blowing on the sails makes a yacht go.

People may eat and sleep on their cabin cruisers on a long trip.

ocean liner

ferry boat

barge

speedboat

submarine

oar

leaky rowing-boat

MORE BOATS

Mr. Fixit's **boat** has a hole in the bottom.
Water is coming in through the hole
and filling the **boat**. It will sink.
Mr. Fixit is drilling another hole
because he thinks the water will
empty out through it. Isn't he silly?

a singing gondolier

gondola

Tugboat Tom

TUGBOAT TOM WAS
BRINGING A BIG SHIP
INTO THE HARBOUR

SUDDENLY
HE HEARD A CRY
FOR HELP!

WAS IT A SAILING-BOAT SINKING?
NO!

WAS IT A CARGO SHIP
CUT IN TWO?
NO! GUESS WHAT!.....

IT WAS BIG HILDA!
SHE HAD GONE OUT
TOO FAR ON HER
TOY HORSE!

SHE IS BIG ENOUGH
TO KNOW BETTER
THAN TO DO THAT.
ISN'T SHE?

GOOD LUCK IN ROME

Federico and Maria were visiting Rome for the very first time. They had heard of a fountain which is supposed to bring you good luck if you throw a coin into it.

Federico stopped his car and got out to ask two carabinieri how to get there.

Now for some reason which can't be explained . . .

... Federico's car started off without him! Maria didn't know how to stop it!
"Follow that car!" Federico said to a taxi driver.

"Help! Help!" said Maria.

Into St. Peter's Square the little car raced.
The Swiss Guards were called out to stop it.
But they were too late.

Down the Spanish Steps
they tumbled.

Down narrow streets . . .
. . . into the very fountain they were looking for.

"You will surely have good luck," said the carabinieri. "Most people have good luck by putting only a penny in the fountain. But look! You have put your car in! Yes, you will surely have good luck!"

231

THE FIREMEN TO THE RESCUE

rescue truck

police car

nozzle

fire engine

rear-wheel steerer

hook-and-ladder truck

hose

front-wheel steerer

boots

helmet

first-aid kit

hook

fire-alarm

A beautiful lady is screaming at her
window. Her house is on fire!
Clang clang! The fire engines,
filled with brave firemen,
are coming to the rescue.

ambulance

water

flames

smoke

fire chief

megaphone

fire chief's car

beautiful
screaming
lady

brave hero

pumper

fire hydrant

jumping
gentleman

ladder

firemen

rescue net

fire
extinguisher

Look at the hero climbing the ladder.
I think he will be able to save
the beautiful lady, don't you?

THINGS WE DO

There are many things
that we can do. And there
are some things we cannot do.
What is one thing we can't do?
Look and see.

dig

build

break

sleep

walk

run

stand

read

watch

kick

pull

push

talk

listen

shout

whisper

laugh

smile

cry

jump over

crawl under

fall down

we can't fly

tip a hat

eat

go up

go down

go in

come out

THE COUNTRY MOUSE

AND THE CITY MOUSE

Told by Patricia Scarry

Annie Mouse lived quietly in the country. One day her friend from the city came to visit her. Annie was delighted.

"Melissa dear, welcome to the country!" she said. "Do come in!"

Annie Mouse asked some friends in for lunch. But Melissa did not eat one nibble of the meal Annie proudly served.

"In the city I dine on spice cake and wine," said the city mouse, rather grandly.

"In the city I have
a machine that plays
music, and I dance
on a velvet carpet,"
said Melissa.

"Oh Annie, won't you leave this dull country
life behind, and come to the city with me?"

"My, it does sound tempting," said Annie.

So Annie rode off to the city with her friend.
Honk! Honk! Beep! Beep! Toot! Toot!
"Please drive slowly," begged Annie.
"Can't hear a word," screamed Melissa.
"Isn't it marvellous fun?"

Melissa's home in the city was beautiful. And such fun to explore! Gaily they raced down the hall.

Suddenly, WHOOF! barked a fierce, angry voice.

"Help! It's the dog!" squeaked Melissa.

And the two friends ran, shaking with fright.

They slammed the dining-room door, just in time. The poor country mouse almost fainted with fear.

But Melissa said, "Oh, he chases me all the time. Come Annie, climb up on the table, beside me. Have you ever seen such food?"

"Never!" gasped Annie, shaking with fright.

There were dainty bits of spice cake, and fine cheese, and even a drop of wine in the glasses.

"OOooh! I am seeing things," squeaked Annie suddenly. "I see a cat!"

"It *is* a cat!" cried Melissa. "Run! Run!"

They slammed the living-room door, just in time.

"Oh!" sobbed Annie. "I have never been so frightened!"

"Nonsense, you'll get used to it," said Melissa. "There, I've put on the music machine. Would you care to dance?"

"No thank you," said Annie and she started to run.

"Annie, where are you going?" called Melissa.

"Home, to the country," squeaked Annie. "Goodbye, Melissa. Thank you for the very nice time. Oh! Help! Oh! Oh! Oh!"

The little mouse ran through the city. She ran and ran and ran. And she did not stop until she was safe in the quiet green country.

That night she told her gentle friends, "I would rather lead a simple life in peace, than dine on riches and live in fear."

MUSIC MAKING

The conductor leads the orchestra by waving his baton. The musicians are playing a very gay tune.
Which of the musical instruments do you think you could learn to play?

double bass

bassoon

cello

oboe

clarinet

piccolo

flute

violin

baton

conductor

piano

podium

248

side drum

bass drum

cymbals

triangle

French horn

trumpet

tuba

cornet

tambourine

trombone

guitar

harp

comb and
tissue paper

harmonica

Trains

This locomotive is called "Puffing Billy." It was made in England.

The "Dewitt Clinton" was an early American train.

The "Lafayette" was another early American locomotive.

Later on, this type of locomotive was seen in the American West.

This was the first locomotive to have six sets of driving wheels.

Oldtime trains were very gaily painted.

This shunter is used on the docks of a busy port.

Modern steam locomotives are being replaced by Diesel and electric engines.

This is a European steam engine pulling a small goods wagon.

Notice the bumpers on these trains.
This is a Diesel engine pulling a tanker.

The engine on a rack railway has a toothed wheel which fits into a toothed rail. This is how it pulls itself up steep mountains.

The Diesel engine is used to pull either freight or passenger trains.

The electric locomotive is used
around big cities and where there
are long tunnels, as it gives off no smoke.

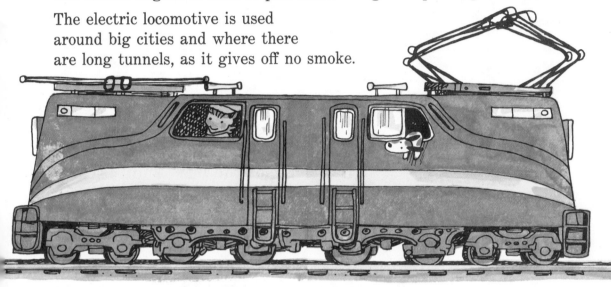

This passenger carriage has its own motor and is used for short runs.

This electric locomotive gets its power from the wire overhead.

COMPAGNIE DES WAGONS-LITS ET DES GRANDS EXPRESS EUROPEENS

SNCF   90

VOITURE - LITS   SLEEPING CAR

MORE TRAINS

rear

Annie Ant is walking forward.

Father Cat

front

Dingo

ahead

behind

Haggis

Pa Pig

Driver

under

Squeaky

The driver is at the front of the bus. Haggis Dog is at the back of the bus. Annie Ant is walking forward to the front of the bus. Pa Pig is sitting backwards, facing the rear of the bus. Father Cat is behind the bus. Who is ahead of the bus? Who is under it?

Diesel passenger train

gondola car with brakeman's cab

signal

What is Dingo trying to do? Does he think he is a train? Get off those railway tracks at once, Dingo!

tracks

Everyone is hurrying to the railway station to catch a train.

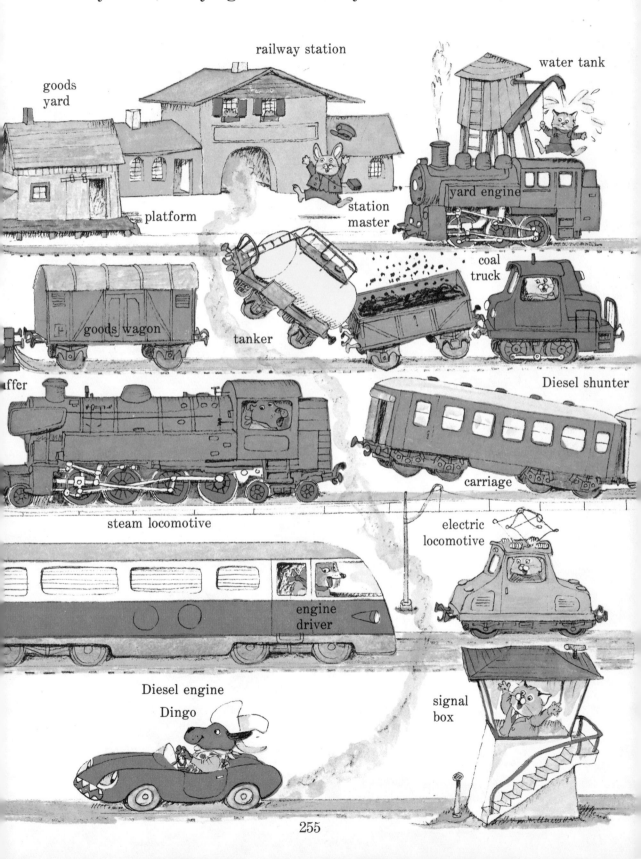

railway station

water tank

goods yard

station master

yard engine

platform

coal truck

goods wagon

tanker

Diesel shunter

ffer

carriage

steam locomotive

electric locomotive

engine driver

Diesel engine
Dingo

signal box

Polite Puppy

POLITE PUPPY SAYS,
"BOW WOW, HOW DO YOU DO?"
WHEN HE MEETS SOMEONE.

HE OPENS DOORS
FOR LADIES.

HE SAYS,
"BOW WOW, THANK YOU,"
WHEN HE IS GIVEN SOMETHING.

HE SAYS," BOW WOW, PLEASE,"
WHEN HE ASKS
FOR SOMETHING.
AND - WHEN HE EATS
HIS MEALS, HE.........

.... OH! THAT NAUGHTY PUPPY!
HE HAS FORGOTTEN
HIS MANNERS!

YOU DON'T SIT IN YOUR DISH
WHEN YOU EAT YOUR MEALS.
DO YOU?

THE DOG AND HIS BONE

told by
Patricia Scarry

A little dog hurried to the stream with a large juicy bone in his mouth. He wanted to eat the bone all by himself. So he ran across a log that bridged the stream.

Then, in the water, he saw a picture of himself. But he thought it was another dog.

"Ah, now I shall have two nice bones to eat," thought the greedy little dog.

He growled, and snapped at the other bone.

SPLASH! His bone fell in the water. And so did he! Now he had nothing to eat.

Greedy-greedy makes a hungry puppy!

THE ALWAYS HUNGRY VISITORS

Mother Cat bought food at the grocery shop. She brought it home and put it on the kitchen table.

Look behind you, Mother Cat! You have some hungry visitors.

ham

steak

jam

roast beef

minced meat

mustard

jelly

sausage

raisins

bacon

frankfurters

soup

ketchup

prunes

bologna/baloney

butter

cheese

peanut butter

milk

a dozen eggs

a pint of cream

strawberry

ice
cream

cake

cereal

buns

spaghetti

coa

salt

biscuits

Mother Cat gave the visitors
a jar of jam to eat.
Where did they ever learn
their table manners?

After they had eaten
they all took naps.

ZZZZZZZZZZ

hammer

nail

TOOLS

Everyone is very busy
working with his tools.
Who always carries his
tool with him?
He has a red head.

push pin

carpenter

board

ladder

sandpaper

sawdust

hacksaw

drill

plane

woodpecker

vice

wood shavings

jig saw

screwdriver

screws

pliers

file

bow saw

trowel

brick-layer

brick wall

brick

timber

fence painter

paint brush

ball of twine

saw horse

barrel

paint

tack

tack hammer

ruler

folding ruler

jackknife

tool box

putty knife

shovel

bolt

nut

earth

compass

wheelbarrow

pickaxe

More Mother Goose Rhymes

Little maid, pretty maid, whither goest thou?
Down in the meadow to milk my cow.
Shall I go with thee? No, not now;
When I send for thee, then come thou.

As I was going to St. Ives,
I met a man with seven wives.
Each wife had seven sacks,
Each sack had seven cats,
Each cat had seven kits;
Kits, cats, sacks, and wives,
How many were there
    going to St. Ives?

Jack Sprat could eat no fat,
His wife could eat no lean,
And so between them both,
    you see,
They licked the platter clean.

TREES

twig

branch

stem

leaf

leaves

apple

tree trunk

Some **trees** bear fruit which is good to eat.
MacIntosh Dog is shaking apples out of the apple **tree**.
Be careful you do not shake anything else out, MacIntosh!

hatchet

axe

bow saw

Chips is chopping down
a **tree**. I hope he gets out
of the way before it falls on him!

woods

saw

board

roots

Trees grow in the woods.
Trees are made of wood.
Chips chopped down the tree.
He is sawing it into boards.

axe

chair

stump

branch

log

jackknife

Chips is sawing the thick branch.

saw

Mr. Fixit is sawing the thin branch.
I wonder who will be the first to finish?

EGG
IN THE
HOLE

One day, up in the hayloft of the barn, Henny laid an egg.
The egg rolled through a hole in the floor to a room down below.
"Oh my! I hope I haven't lost it!" she said.

Henny rushed down the stairs to the room below.

"Have you seen my egg?" asked Henny.

"Yes, I have," said Billy Goat. "It fell on my ice cream.
Then it rolled along the table and went out the window."

Henny hurried to the window.

"Have you seen my egg?" she asked.

"Yes, I have," said Little Bird.

"It rolled along the rain gutter and then went down the hole."

Henny ran outside where Pig was sitting.

"Have you seen my egg?" asked Henny. "I'm afraid I have lost it."

"Your egg just hit me on the head," said Pig. "It rolled down my back, through my curly tail, and across the barnyard."

Henny rushed across the barnyard.

She saw her egg just before it rolled into a hole in the ground.

Just then from out of the hole appeared a tiny mouse.

"Henny," he said, "I have found your egg! Something very special happened . . . It is broken and it is in a lot of little pieces BUT . . .

if you look closely . . .

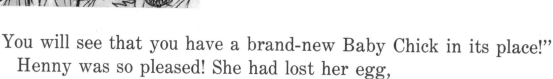

You will see that you have a brand-new Baby Chick in its place!"

Henny was so pleased! She had lost her egg, but now she had a baby chick instead.

You would be too, wouldn't you?

"Hello, Mummy," said Baby Chick.

SCHTOOMPAH,
THE FUNNY AUSTRIAN

Schtoompah was a funny fellow.
He was not very tidy. Instead
of putting things away neatly,
he would just throw things
in a cupboard.

He threw his tuba in the cupboard.

He threw mittens and jackets
and rakes into that cupboard.

He even threw his television set in
by mistake.

And then when he went to look for
something he could never find it.

Schtoompah was going to play his
tuba for the Saturday night band
concert. He spent two whole days
looking for his tuba before he
finally found it.

Now, he was ready to go to the
band concert.

Schtoompah put his tuba on his head, and rode his bicycle backwards.

"Oh that Schtoompah, he is a funny fellow," the townspeople all said. "I wonder what funny thing he will do at the band concert?"

The band concert was about to begin.
"Uh-ein, uh-zwei, uh-drei," said the band leader.

Schtoompah blew, but
no music came out.

He blew even harder, but
still no music came out.

Schtoompah took a deep breath;
and blew with all his might. . . .

BLAZZZZZZZZZZZ!

"Oh, that Schtoompah!
He is a funny fellow,"
the townspeople all laughed.

MERRY MONTHS
OF THE YEAR

by Patricia Scarry

❄ JANUARY ❄

January starts the brand-new year with snow for tobogganing, skiing, snowmen. There are icy ponds for skating on.

Mittens drip,
And there's cocoa to sip.
This month there's a nice thing to do:
Throw crumbs to the birds! They're hungry too.

F·E·B·R·U·A·R·Y

February is slushy and short. Only 28 days to play,
Some of them sunny, most of them grey.
Then every four years there is Leap Year, with 29 days.
The best one of all is Valentine's Day.

M·A·R·C·H

March is gusty, muddy, blustery. This is the month
for flying kites, roller-skating, windy nights.

Wear something green on St. Patrick's Day.
Robins sing, "Spring is on the way!"
And bears wake up from their winter's sleep.

A·P·R·I·L

April is fun! The very first day is April Fool's,
a day for playing jokes.

All month long the weather teases.
Now it's warm, then, oops! the sneezes!
Take off your boots and it will shower:
Then the sun shines for an hour.

Robins are nesting, puddles are skiddy, violets pop!

No wonder April's gay and funny—
You know who's coming? The Easter Bunny!

May—and it's time to play outdoors again.
The world is filled with flowers.
> On lawns and hills and window sills
> Are sunny, saucy daffodils!
> And everywhere I hear the sound of little things
> Bravely trying out new wings.
> Ducks are quacky, turtles snappy.
> I think my heart will not be still
> 'til I roll down a grassy hill.

JUNE

June—and school is over soon!
   Then all we'll do each day
   Is play and play—hooray!
   Summer arrives June 21—the nicest day of the year.
   We'll laze on the grass and listen, and hear:
   Bees buzzing! Hummingbirds whirring! Worms wiggling!
   June is laughing, golden, giggling!
   Today I'll visit the brook and dip in my toes.
   I'll perch at the edge, and hope a butterfly lands on
      my nose.

JULY

July begins with a *boom!*
    Sometimes it's thunder,
    With lightning in the sky.
    Sometimes it's the rummy-tum-tum
    Of a drummer marching by.
You can get dressed up and carry flags,
And play in your very own band.
And now is the time to make cold drinks
To sell at your lemonade stand.
    At night, if you see a star fall, *swiiish!*
    Be sure to make a lovely wish.

A·U·G·U·S·T

August is steamy, hot, ice-creamy.
  Maybe you'll visit the seashore . . .
  Play under the garden hose . . .
  Swing in the hammock with bare toes.
Summer is nearly over, and birds stay up late.
Suppers are hot-dogs, cooked out of doors—
  So good you can hardly wait!

SEPTEMBER

September is new shoes, and back to school.
Berries are ripening, apples turn red.
Nuts are browning. It's early to bed.
Squirrels are storing their nuts away.
Days are short; there's less time to play.
Autumn's here. The summer's gone.
Better put your sweater on.

O·C·T·O·B·E·R

October is orange and red and brown.
See the leaves all tumble down!
    Rake them up into piles so high
    You can jump in them, and flop, and lie.
Now the farmer harvests his hay.
The barn is filled. And every day is growing shorter.
We have to wait the whole long month for
    spooky Hallowe'en.
What are you going to be? A ghost? A witch?
    Or a queen?

NOVEMBER

November smells of turkey, grapes, and pumpkin pie,
And leaf-smoke curling gently into the sky.
Some animals have burrowed into the earth
To sleep until the spring.
Is a cricket sharing your house for the winter?
Can you hear him sing?
Nature's garden is resting.
The trees are stark and bare.
Now you can see the lovely nests
You didn't know were there.

DECEMBER

December is waiting and wanting and wishing
and longing for Christmas Day.
    This is the merriest month of all—
    Make decorations to hang in the hall,
    A fairy to sit on the tree,
    Hide presents in places where none can see.
We try to be as good as gold all month, so very good,
because we know who's coming down the chimney—
    Jolly Santa Claus!

More Mother Goose Rhymes

I see the moon, and the moon sees me.
God bless the moon, and God bless me.

Star light, star bright,
First star I see tonight,
I wish I may, I wish I might,
Have the wish I wish tonight.

Twinkle, twinkle, little star,
How I wonder what you are!
Up above the world so high,
Like a diamond in the sky.

When the blazing sun is gone,
When he nothing shines upon,
Then you show your little light,
Twinkle, twinkle, all the night.

Good night,
Sleep tight,
Wake up bright
In the morning light,
To do what's right
With all your might

LOOK! Who is that riding home on his bicycle?
WHY! It is Schtoompah!
He has drawn a funny face on his tuba.
My, he is a funny fellow!
I hope he remembers to put his tuba away
neatly, in his cupboard, don't you?
Do you ever forget to put your tuba away
in your cupboard, before you go to bed?
Do you?

THE END